CLIMATE CHANGE

HARRIET BRUNDLE

PROTECTING OUR
PLANET

©2018
Book Life
King's Lynn
Norfolk PE30 4LS

ISBN: 978-1-78637-266-6

Written by:
Harriet Brundle

Edited by:
Kirsty Holmes

Designed by:
Gareth Liddington

A catalogue record for this book
is available from the British Library.

Photocredits: Abbreviations: l-left, r-right, b-bottom, t-top, c-centre, m-middle. All images are courtesy of Shutterstock.com.

Covert – Paraksa, Coverm – Marten_House, Coverb – Bernhard Staehli, 1l – Kotomiti Okuma, 1r – Iakov Filimonov, 2 – IrinaK, 3 – Sponner, 4l – Siriwat Chamnanyoch, 4r – Martin Sistek, 5 – Yusiki, 6 – kwest, 7 – manfredxy, 8 – ChameleonsEye, 9 – ssuaphotos, 10tl – Hung Chung Chih, 10tr – The Clay Machine Gun, 10bl – Gubin Yury, 10br – Sokolenko, 11 – Ints Vikmanis, 12 – geckoz, 13 – WitthayaP, 14 – Rich Carey, 15 – Phanumassu Sang-ngam, 17 – Dr Morley Read, 18 – Horst Lieber, 19 – FloridaStock, 20 – Ekaterina Pokrovsky, 21 – Volodymyr Goinyk, 22 – Olga Danylenko, 23 – Jozef Sowa, 24 – Rich Carey.

Images are courtesy of Shutterstock.com. With thanks to Getty Images, Thinkstock Photo and iStockphoto.

CONTENTS

Words that look like **this** can be found in the glossary on page 24.

WHAT DOES
CLIMATE MEAN?

'Weather' is what we call the day-to-day changes we see outside, like rain or **temperature**. The weather may change every day or even within the same day.

The climate is the usual weather of a place over a longer period of time. Antarctica, for example, has extremely cold weather for most of the year. California has mostly sunny and warm weather.

CALIFORNIA, USA

ANTARCTICA

WHAT IS
CLIMATE CHANGE?

When there is a **long-term** change in the usual weather for a place, we call it 'climate change'.

WE CAN USE A RAIN GAUGE TO MEASURE HOW MUCH RAIN HAS FALLEN.

Climate change can cause more or less rain to fall than expected over a year. Or it could cause the temperature of a particular place to be much higher or lower, for a long period of time.

GLOBAL
WARMING

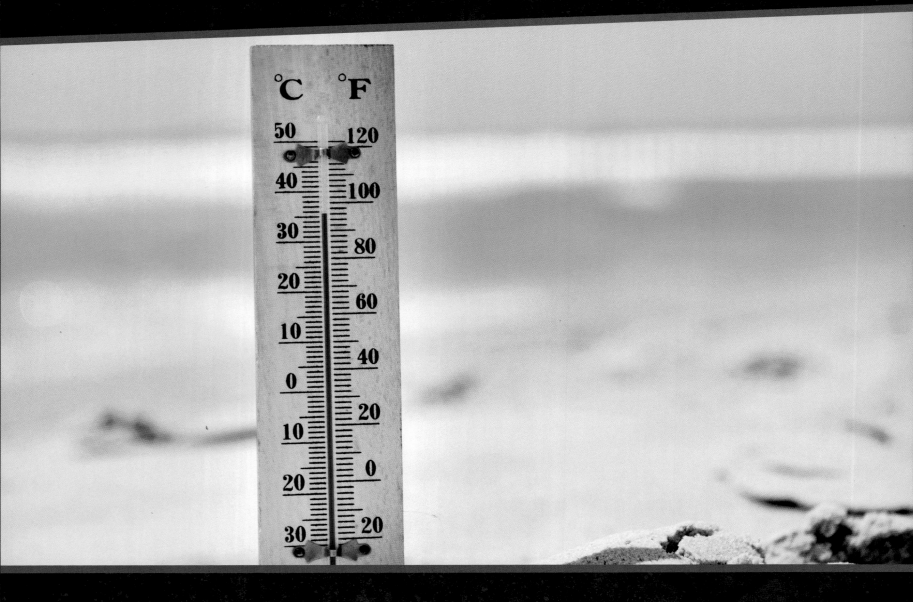

Global warming is the long-term rise in the temperature on Earth. Even the smallest change in the Earth's temperature can cause huge changes for our planet.

Global warming is caused by harmful **gases** which are being released into the Earth's **atmosphere**. This is mostly happening because of things that humans are doing.

CARS RELEASE HARMFUL GASES.

POLLUTION

When something is added to the **environment** that has a harmful effect, it is called pollution. There are lots of different types of pollution.

AIR POLLUTION

WATER POLLUTION

HEAT POLLUTION

SOIL POLLUTION

ANY TYPE OF POLLUTION CAN BE DANGEROUS FOR THE ENVIRONMENT.

As there are more and more people on the planet, we are causing more and more pollution. This is bad for the environment.

AIR POLLUTION

FOSSIL FUELS ARE BURNED TO MAKE ELECTRICITY.

When **fossil fuels** are burned, harmful gases like **carbon dioxide** are added to the air. This causes air pollution.

Having lots of carbon dioxide and other harmful gases in the air is speeding up global warming. This is damaging the planet.

SOLAR PANELS AND WIND TURBINES HELP THE PLANET BECAUSE THEY MAKE ELECTRICITY WITHOUT RELEASING HARMFUL GASES.

DEFORESTATION

When large areas of forest are cut down, it is called deforestation. Trees are cut down to make more space for humans to live or to make things like paper and furniture.

THE WOOD THAT HAS BEEN CUT DOWN MAY BE BURNED. THIS RELEASES CARBON DIOXIDE WHICH CAUSES AIR POLLUTION.

Trees use up carbon dioxide, which is a harmful gas, and release oxygen, which is a useful gas. This helps to lower levels of air pollution. If the trees have been cut down, this cannot happen.

THE AMAZON RAINFOREST

SOUTH AMERICA

The Amazon **Rainforest** in South America is the world's biggest rainforest. It is home to millions of animals and plants.

In recent years, nearly 20% of the Amazon Rainforest has been destroyed by deforestation. It is now being used as space for humans to keep cows.

THE AMAZON RAINFOREST

WHAT ARE THE EFFECTS OF CLIMATE CHANGE?

Climate change causes the weather to become more extreme. We may see **droughts**, storms, floods or heat waves.

EXTREME WEATHER CAN AFFECT THE AMOUNT OF FOOD WE ARE ABLE TO GROW.

Climate change is also affecting animals that cannot **adjust** fast enough to the rising temperatures. Animals that use the temperature as a sign to tell them when to **migrate** are becoming confused and starting their journeys at the wrong time.

Global warming means that ice in places like Antarctica is melting, and this extra water is being added to the oceans. This causes heavy floods

Penguins and polar bears that live on the ice could be left without enough space to live as the ice slowly melts away.

HOW CAN WE HELP?

You could help by planting a tree. Trees release oxygen and use up some of the gases that cause global warming. You could plant a new tree in your garden at home, or at school.

With the help of an adult, try to find out about what others in your local area are doing to help stop climate change, and try to get involved yourself.

Rather than using the car, try to walk or cycle to where you want to go. If you have to travel in a car, you could try sharing with others who are also going to the same place, or use the bus.

Tell your friends and family all about climate change and how important it is to look after our planet. They might be interested in helping to make a change too!

GLOSSARY AND INDEX

GLOSSARY

adjust	to change
atmosphere	the mixture of gases that make up the air and surround the Earth
carbon dioxide	a natural, colourless gas that is found in the air
droughts	a long period of very little rainfall, which leads to a lack of water
environment	the natural world
fossil fuels	fuels, such as coal, oil and gas, that formed millions of years ago from the remains of animals and plants
gases	air-like substances that expand freely to fill any space available
long-term	happening over a long period of time
migrate	move from one place to another based on seasonal changes
rainforest	a large forest that experiences lots of rainfall
temperature	how hot or cold a person, place or object is

INDEX